COMPANION
PLANTED

COMPANION
PLANTED

Imagining the Depths
and Fruits of
Discipleship

RICK SHAFER

Scripture quotations are from Revised Standard Version of the Bible,
copyright © 1946, 1952, and 1971 National Council of the Churches of
Christ in the United States of America. All rights reserved worldwide.

Printed in the United States of America

Library of Congress Control Number: 2022916232

Paperback ISBN: 979-8-9866949-0-0
Ebook ISBN: 979-8-9866949-2-4

Storylines United Media
Wilmington, North Carolina USA
storylinesunited.com

FOR MY GRANDCHILDREN

You see to a thousand generations.

Help me see three.

In my imagination, picture the church

    that our children's children will be.

What seeds will You have me sow?

In what soil will they germinate and grow?

When I am weak, will everyone see

    that, just for a moment, my eyes were on me?

And that when I am strong,

    it was You all along?

Your child and Your gifts, it's to You these belong.

You see to a thousand generations.

Help me see three.

ORIENTATION

There are a great many books and resources on Christian discipleship. Some are theologically oriented, covering the basics, catechism style. Others emphasize helpful habits, rhythms, and spiritual practices. And a few give practical exercises for engaging the Church and the world as disciples of Jesus. In my faith formation role, I use and recommend some of these resources.

This is more of an orienting book – orienting disciples to their discipleship. Here I advocate for discipleship – which I define as *training myself and others to be trained by Christ* – to become a lifelong deepening:

1. into our distinctness from the world and in the world,

2. into our oneness as a people, and

3. in our capacity to love.

From that depth, I imagine a corresponding offer of care, connection, and goodness. In my mind, the visual is a tree farm with three great trees, each with a depth and a fruit.

My hope for this little book is that it helps disciples – as migrants from the world's system to God's kingdom – read their Bibles, sit under great writers from across the centuries, and weigh other discipleship resources.

I also hope this book gives direction to our steps. Formation happens when we are vulnerable and willing to take risks. Can our churches provide spaces for disciples to live more distinctly, to be more accepted and accepting, and to do the hard work of loving like Jesus? Said another way, can we risk becoming more authentic specimens of God's redemptive community in the world?

ACKNOWLEDGEMENTS

I am quick to say I've never had an original thought. That might not be entirely true; I shouldn't blame others for some of the stuff that comes out. But I am keenly aware that I've been influenced by a cloud of witnesses – so many of whom I can't credit here. I can mention a few. First, thanks to my wife, Elizabeth, for showing me what a life of worship and faith looks like. Who else would have willingly and lovingly journeyed with me as you have? To paraphrase a greeting card, love grows where you're planted. Likewise, thank you to Tom, Martha, Daniel, and Brenda for your gifts of love, patience, and encouragement. From my missions days, there are so many to thank. But I especially want to thank Bob, Phil, and Mark for all those conversations that mattered. To friends working in the nations, thank you. I am grateful to my pastor, Mike Ashcraft, to Richie Marshall and the leadership team, and to the staff of Port City Community Church for giving me a place to grow and experiment. What a gift. Thanks to our Friends and Followers small group for your curiosity and authenticity. Above all, I am grateful to you, God, for your grace to me: for all these people you've placed in my life, for those who came before and loved future generations enough to write, for the path you've given me to walk, and for your mercies that are new every morning. Great is your faithfulness.

OUR TREE FARM

Imagine with me a tree farm. It's a different sort of farm with lots of residents – like neighbors in a golf community. Where the golf community is quiet – but for the curses shouted into the wind – our farm is vibrant and full of life. Birds singing. Bees buzzing. Tractors pulling trailers. Children running and laughing. Community picnics with lots of pie. And cute farm animals organized petting zoo style. People who live here dwell in *shalom*, an active peace. Nothing is withheld; everything and everyone are rightly related. Our farm is wonderful but it's not always serene. We're tested by harsh storms and pressures from the edges. In these squalls our trees grow stronger. And so do we. As you read, will you use your imagination and make this place home for a while?

Our farm might be known for many things, but its trees steal the show. Three trees, companion planted, define us. If you aren't familiar with the term, companion planting is the farming technique of growing complementary plants together for their mutual benefit. In the natural world, companioned plants increase pollination, improve the soil and its structure, reduce insect damage, protect against strong winds, and regulate sunlight.

On our imagined farm, three select trees are planted together: Holiness, Wholeness, and Purpose. The vitality of our community is tied to the depth and fruitfulness of these trees. And it's to their maturity that we give our energies. Let's study each one. Let's discover their nature and learn what they require to grow strong, healthy, and fruitful.

THE HOLINESS TREE

You shall be holy to me; for I the Lord am holy, and have separated you from the peoples, that you should be mine.

(Lev. 20:26)

A DEPTH OF HOLINESS

Our first tree – the one I will give most attention to – is Holiness (*hagios* in the Greek). Maybe you cringe at the thought of Holiness being the anchor tree on our farm. Holiness seems like an old-fashioned tree, overlooked by many for some *du jour* variety. What do you think of when you hear the word holy? Holy Bible? Holier than thou? Head coverings, robes, and hushed voices? Or maybe stifling legalism?

This magnificent tree gradually lost popularity as its true nature was distorted and mostly forgotten. You might be surprised to learn that the word 'holy' means something quite different from puckered-up or self-righteous. Holy means:

- called out

- set apart for a particular purpose

- different, distinct, or peculiar

The Holiness tree is unlike any other. It's grand – imposing even – taller than the rest. It instinctively reaches to the heavens, branches raised and secure, unmoved by both admirers and critics.

Our tree isn't just distinct, it's distinct in ways that God is distinct. A place can be called holy if it is set aside for God's purpose. In the Bible, we see this in the tabernacle and temple where we find the Holy Place and Most Holy Place, or Holy of Holies. We see it when a piece of turf is named holy ground. Objects are called holy when they are set apart as God's.

Yes, holiness can refer to places and things, but on our farm the Holiness tree stands for a holy *people* – a people who are called by God's name – a people who are holy (distinct from all other peoples) in ways that God is holy.

In the Old Testament, God made the people of Israel holy, calling them out from all the peoples of the earth. God gave them laws, feasts, customs, and rituals to unite them and to distinguish them from everyone else. Israel was to be the pattern that all other nations and tribes could look at and see life centered on the One True God.

In the New Testament, this invitation to Holiness was extended to non-Jews. In Jesus, we Gentiles could now be grafted into God's holy vine (Rom. 11:16-20). We were invited to be members of this called out, set apart, distinct, peculiar society. Scripture tells us that those who abide in this vine (John 15) are called saints. Note that, in the Greek, the same root word is used for *saints* (a noun) as is used for *holy* (an adjective). Saints are all of us 'called out ones' who are set apart as God's.

Since we're people who are holy in ways that God is holy, the word *godliness* is closely related. Godliness defines what we should look like when we live as holy people in the same direction that God is holy. And what do holy, godly people look like? For us to serve as an image to the world, we needed an example of our own. Providentially, there is One who is that example: One who said, "If you have seen me, you have seen the Father" (John 14:9), and "I and the Father are one" (John 10:30). Jesus is God incarnate: 'God with skin on'. We don't have to guess what godliness looks like. We see it perfectly in Jesus. Jesus is what God is like. The way of Jesus is what godliness looks like.

As I reflect on godliness, I remember the difficulty I once had with something Jesus taught in his Sermon on the Mount (Matt. 5:13). First, he told his followers – his disciples – that they were to be the salt of the earth but then went on to say that if salt loses its saltiness, it is useless. What? Being trained as a chemical engineer, I have learned that salt (sodium chloride) is a very stable compound! Salt doesn't just lose its saltiness! It took John Stott [1] to show me that the way salt can lose its saltiness is by dilution. Mix enough non-salt with salt and its saltiness will fade. What Jesus was saying to his followers is this: people were originally made – and his followers have been remade – to be holy in ways that God is holy. Our godliness will have an effect on the surrounding culture to the degree that we aren't contaminated – diluted – by the world's systems, structures, and patterns.

[1] John R. W. Stott, *Reading the Sermon on the Mount*, IVP Connect, July 25, 2016

RESCUED AND RESETTLED

- ◉ -

How do we become holy? From Genesis we know that Adam and Eve were banished from the Garden of Eden because of sin. From then on, they and their descendants inhabited a broken world. That's the world we have been born into. We start off as part of that world. And on our own we are unable to change. But God in his mercy made a way. Look at Colossians 1:13-14:

> [The Father] has rescued us from the power of darkness and transferred us into the kingdom of his beloved Son, in whom we have redemption, the forgiveness of sins.

Following my junior year of high school, my family moved to a different city, 275 miles away. Like any kid probably, I dreaded having to start over just a year before graduation. But in hindsight, I can see that I was rescued from a place that wasn't so great for me and transferred to someplace better. Better grades. Healthier friendships. A sense of direction, with accountability. This new city was also where I met my wife!

In this Colossians passage, the apostle Paul is writing "to the saints and faithful brothers and sisters in Christ" (v.1). The saints are a called out, set apart, holy people – a community, or family of brothers and sisters, who have placed their faith in Jesus. These, the Father has rescued and transferred – or as I like to say – resettled.

The Father has rescued us. We were born into a broken world – a world that lies outside God's garden, beyond intimate fellowship with our Creator. And there is nothing we can do on our own to restore that relationship. The 'power of darkness' rules us; we are slaves to it.

But we see that God, in Jesus, rescued us from this power of darkness. Through his death and resurrection, this power has been defeated and our bondage has been broken. The gates of our captivity have been demolished and just outside is restored fellowship with the Father – the fellowship God originally intended – the fellowship we were created for. This freedom is available to all. Who will receive it?

Again, in his letter to the Colossians, Paul is writing directly to those who have bowed their hearts to God, have placed their faith in Jesus, and have taken this step of faith from bondage to freedom. Paul's message is for every disciple (student or apprentice) of Jesus, then and now. How does it feel to be rescued? Were you aware that you needed to be rescued? Rescued from what? Rescued to what?

The Father has rescued us. He's also resettled us. Not only were believers rescued from the power of darkness, we've been transferred to another kingdom – the kingdom of God's Son. From the rule of darkness to the rule of light. From the way of death to the way of life. This resettlement is as dramatic as a change of national residency. More dramatic in fact. The Bible uses metaphors like a change of citizenship, or adoption into a new family, to help us imagine the comprehensive, all-immersive shift this resettlement entails. This is how metaphors work. Illustrations we can relate to – like citizenship and adoption – help us imagine realities we can't fully grasp. The Bible is full of metaphors like these.

Finishing out these two verses in Colossians, we see that, just as we were rescued and resettled, we were also redeemed and forgiven our sins.

The Father redeemed us. We were slaves to sin. We were owned by sin. We were the property of sin. But by Jesus' death and resurrection we have been rescued. By our faith in Jesus' death, resurrection, and authority, we have been resettled and we are God's family now. We belong to him. Of course, that transfer of ownership came at a price – a price Jesus paid on the cross.

The Father also forgave our sins. We might think that God's redemption of us resulted in a debt that we now owe to him. But it's a debt he has forgiven. We've been released from that debt and God remembers it no more. Our only debt now is a debt of gratitude and love. We are forgiven and we've been reconciled to the Father. We are invited into his household. We are his family. We are his friends by his choice and grace.

We were made holy when we placed faith in Jesus' death, resurrection, and authority. God rescued us and, with our profession of allegiance to him, he redeemed us, resettled us, and forgave us.

FAITH, BELIEF, AND MISSING THE MARK

I've made references to sin but haven't defined it. Recall Adam's and Eve's sin in the Garden. They ate the fruit of the Tree of the Knowledge of Good and Evil, when God had instructed them not to. Was this just a matter of eating a piece of forbidden fruit? Sin in the Garden resulted in their banishment from the Garden; a pretty harsh punishment for eating a piece of fruit that was a 'delight to the eyes'. They were banished to a world where sin reigns. See, sin is not just an action, it's also a governance. In Colossians, we saw that this rule of sin is called a power – or a dominion – of darkness. Sin is a governance we are born into, and are ruled by, until we enter our freedom in Christ by faith.

The Biblical understanding of sin (*hamartia* in the Greek) is borrowed from the world of archery. It's 'missing the mark'. It's not just missing the bullseye; it's missing the center of the bullseye. Any deviation is sin.

One of my favorite jobs during college days was working as a surveyor. I would look through the transit – a scope on a tripod – and align to a target. I had to make sure the transit was perfectly level because, as I was reminded often, a small deviation up close will result in a big error down the road.

So, what is the disciple's target? We find an answer in something the apostle Paul writes in half a verse found in Romans:

...for whatever does not proceed from faith is sin (Rom. 14:23b).

The target is *everything that proceeds from faith.* And what is faith? My definition of faith is 'trust that's able to take a step'. The Greek word for faith (*pistis*) is sometimes translated as 'belief'. Using my definition for faith (and belief), we could rewrite the Romans verse this way:

...for whatever does not proceed from [trust that's able to take a step] is sin (Rom. 14:23b).

Then there's Hebrews 11:6, where we find this same root word translated as both *faith* and *believe*:

And without *faith* it is impossible to please [God]. For whoever would draw near to God must *believe* that he exists and that he rewards those who seek him. (Italicized emphasis mine)

Faith in God is trust in his limitless and unchanging love, knowledge, wisdom, goodness, care, power, provision, presence – and everything else he reveals of himself in Creation, Scripture, and Jesus. It's trust in his royal authority and his father-heart. It's trust in his message. But *what* we trust must flow from *who* we trust. Faith is relational. Our faith is in God, not just the things we've learned *about* him. There are many more 'whats' to discover and to experience in new ways. But there's only one 'who'. *Who* do you trust?

Adam and Eve were created to trust God. They walked with God in the Garden and enjoyed fellowship with him. But then another voice entered the story. The Serpent asked

Adam and Eve to trust *him*. He deceived them into eating the fruit they were forbidden by God to eat. Eating the fruit was sin, for sure. But the underlying sin was *their failure to trust God*. This is the sin that broke everything. It's the sin Jesus died to rescue us from – this root sin and all its offshoots.

Like Adam and Eve, we too encounter many different voices. We are exposed to so many competing and inconsistent philosophies about who we are and how we should live. So where do we place our trust? Which voice governs us? That is the ultimate question of faith, belief, and sin. Of course, in our humanness, we are going to miss the target sometimes, but it's important to know what the target is and to keep that target in our sights.

If what does not proceed from faith is sin, then faith is most important to godliness – something we see in Scripture from Genesis to Revelation. Faith in God is trust in God. It's a kind of trust that plays out in our choices and actions. James chapter 2 tells us that faith without works is dead faith. A trust in God that does not produce a Jesus-like (godly) lifestyle, is dead faith. We are resettled by a faith that's alive. We are, in ways that should be obvious to all, holy as God is holy.

Again, this kind of faith is found throughout Scripture. Here are some examples from Hebrews 11, often called the 'Hall of Faith'. I have substituted my definition for the word 'faith':

- By [trust that's able to take a step] Abraham obeyed when he was called to set out for a place that he was to receive as an inheritance; and he set out, not knowing where he was going.

- By [trust that's able to take a step] Moses was hidden by his parents for three months after his birth, because they saw that the child was beautiful; and they were not afraid of the king's edict.

- By [trust that's able to take a step] Moses, when he was grown up, refused to be called a son of Pharaoh's daughter, choosing rather to share ill-treatment with the people of God than to enjoy the fleeting pleasures of sin.

- By [trust that's able to take a step] the people passed through the Red Sea as if it were dry land, but when the Egyptians attempted to do so they were drowned.

- By [trust that's able to take a step] Rahab the prostitute did not perish with those who were disobedient, because she had received the spies in peace.

- Through [trust that's able to take a step], Gideon, Barak, Samson, Jephthah, David, Samuel and the prophets conquered kingdoms, administered justice, obtained promises, shut the mouths of lions, quenched raging fire, escaped the edge of the sword, won strength out of weakness, became mighty in war, and put foreign armies to flight.

- By [trust that's able to take a step] others suffered mocking and flogging, and even chains and imprisonment. They were stoned to death, they were sawn in two, they were killed by the sword; they went about in skins of sheep and goats, destitute, persecuted, tormented. They wandered in deserts and mountains, and in caves and holes in the ground.

Faith's actions and ends are expressed in different ways because faith in God is personal and relational. We aren't promised that our life here will be comfortable, but we can trust God, whatever comes, because he is trustworthy.

Like Adam and Eve, we can also put our faith in wrong things. There are the obvious examples like wealth, power, status, political figures and parties. But then there are some others that are more subtle, like our tendency to control people and events, our dependence on laws, the approval of other people, our popularity, our self-image, and majority opinion. Anything or anyone other than God that gets our ultimate faith is an idol. And as John Calvin famously said, "the human heart is a perpetual idol factory" [2]. We are all prone to lose sight of the true target: trust (in God) that's able to take a step. When we do miss this mark, we must repent – adjust course or maybe turn completely around. We have to redirect our trust back to God in a way that reorients our actual lived life.

Looking at sin this way, we can see how sin will include every behavior that disregards God's authority and how sin is a governance that can rule us. But if we've placed our faith in Jesus, we have been delivered from that governance. In his letters, the apostle Paul reminds us often that we used to be one way but now we are another way. He contrasts the desires of the flesh – residues of the old way of life in the world – with a life led by the Spirit – our new way of life in God's kingdom.

Some people love the book of James because it's so refreshingly practical. Can I suggest that James is practical because faith is practical? The book of James is a book of living faith. The faith James argues for is trust in God that plays itself out in our thought life, motives, decisions, and actions – trust in God that's able to take a step. Any other faith is either dead faith or idolatry. Whatever does not proceed from faith is sin. And our response to sin must be a course correction. We need to adjust our aim to hit the target: living faith; trust in God.

Too often, churches only counsel people to correct wrong thoughts or behaviors. This kind of training may be appropriate for the young but it's insufficient for maturity.

If we only train people to correct their behaviors but don't train them to trust God, we will eventually wear ourselves out. And be disappointed. When Jesus commissioned us to make disciples of all peoples (Matt. 28:18-20), he was calling us to something specific: "Go and recruit people to place their faith in me."

Even good works that do not proceed from faith miss the mark.

> "Not every one who says to me, 'Lord, Lord,' shall enter the kingdom of heaven, but he who does the will of my Father who is in heaven. On that day many will say to me, 'Lord, Lord, did we not prophesy in your name, and cast out demons in your name, and do many mighty works in your name?' And then will I declare to them, 'I never knew you; depart from me, you evildoers.'"
>
> *(Matt. 7:21-23)*

Many people think these are some of the scariest verses in the Bible. But I would like you to feel the freedom in them. Your life in Christ doesn't come from the things you do *apart from* him, or *for* him, but rather the things you do *with* him. He wants to be known. Trust is personal and relational. It involves knowing and being known.

---

[2] John Calvin, *Institutes of the Christian Religion*, 1559

CLARITY AND JUDGMENT

Establishing faith as our target gives us a clarity of aim, but not the exactness of application that we so often want. The verse from Romans 14:

> ...for whatever does not proceed from faith is sin. (Rom. 14:23b)

is set in an interesting context. Paul is writing to believers who have different convictions about things like observing the sabbath day and eating certain foods. He's telling them that each should obey their own conscience because whatever does not proceed from faith is sin. Apparently, people can have different convictions and practices and still be faithful to God. Paul goes on to warn against judging one another over those differences. We're not to criticize other believers because they hold a different view. So, what *should* we do? Let's:

1. encourage one another to humble ourselves before God and to maintain consciences that are responsive to him

2. help each other hear what God has to say

3. expect every believer to trust God

4. live our lives accordingly

5. resist judging practical outcomes and extend love.

We are a distinct people called out of the world to be different from the world in ways that God is different from the world. In Jesus, we have been set free from the broken systems and patterns of this world and have been resettled in God's kingdom – a dominion ruled by Christ. We are no longer slaves to sin. Instead, we are a people who share faith in God – who share a trust in God that orders our whole lives.

TRUST OR PRESUME

God invites us to ask, seek, and knock. In our finiteness and our dependence as humans, we seek God. We bang on his door. And we ask. This is right. It's as things should be. As a holy people, we come to our Father, the King, and make our petitions known. Since God alone possesses all knowledge and wisdom – a perfect perspective – we ask with open hands, prepared for an answer of 'yes', 'no', or 'not yet'. To go beyond this – to take a 'yes' (or 'no') answer for granted – is presumption, not trust. James warns us that we can have wrong motives:

> You ask and do not receive, because you ask wrongly,
> to spend it on your passions. (James 4:3)

My motives aren't always right. It can be perilous to make choices based on presumption. So, I need to order my steps based on trust. God has clearly revealed his greatness, his goodness, his nearness, his unconditional love, and his forgiveness. I see these in Scripture, and I have experienced them in life. These are truths I can trust. I can arrange my life around them. But there are also asks without answers. To presume that God's answer will be what I want to hear – is not trust in God that merits taking a step.

Now faith is the assurance of things hoped for, the conviction of things not seen. (Heb. 11:1)

Things not seen. Humans like to know where we stand; to see where we're going. We want well-defined boxes. Even if we tend to live 'outside the box', we feel the need to see the box. And we make sure everyone else sees the box. But I don't believe God wants us to live in boxes. He wants us to live free – just by his side. With him, much of our time will be in places that seem familiar and safe. But there will be times when he leads us 'to a land I will show you' (Gen. 12:1). It does take faith to live regular life in this world as a peculiar people. But faith grows most 'out there' – beyond what's absolute, settled, and seen. There are segments of our journey where the only thing we can hang onto is trust. We face complexity, confusion, charges leveled by the Accuser and accusers, and questions – lots of questions. No boxes here. Don't be presumptuous. Hear from God and trust him step by step.

MANIFOLD GRACE

Our Holiness didn't just happen. And it wasn't our work either. It was the Father who rescued us and resettled us. It's God who every moment enables us to live in this new kingdom. These are gifts to us – his grace to us. Allow me to share my definition of this word grace (*Charis* in the Greek):

> Grace is the unmerited God-given desire, ability, and resources to participate in our Father's economy (purpose, plan, activity) as His beloved.

Grace is God's gift, given in many forms, to an undeserving people. For one full year I made a concerted effort to name God's gifts of grace to me. What have I received from him that I did not earn? I'm confident that if you try this too, you'll find it as overwhelming as I did. Any desire we have to trust God, any ability we have to take a step towards him or with him, is his gift to us. Apart from God's grace we are without hope. But his grace is always abundant, sufficient, and available. We need only to receive it and trust him to govern our lives. Living by God's grace takes discipline and hard work, but his grace is a gift. As Dallas Willard said,

Grace is not opposed to effort, it is opposed to earning. Earning is attitude, effort is action.[3]

[3] Dallas Willard, *The Great Omission: Reclaiming Jesus's Essential Teachings on Discipleship*, HarperOne, May 14, 2014

BORN ANEW

Imagine you are resettled to another country – maybe by your own choice, or maybe not. By resettled I mean your citizenship has changed. Or imagine you are adopted into a new family. These are dramatic, comprehensive, immersive life changes. And both are biblical metaphors for what happens when we move from the dominion of darkness into the kingdom of God's Son. Everything is new. Everything.

> For those who are in Christ Jesus,
> a new heart. A new spirit.
> a new citizenship. A new family.
> a new Sovereign and Father.
> a new identity and culture.

Hear the apostle Paul say it in his letter to the Corinthians:

> Therefore, if any one is in Christ, he is a new creation; the old has passed away, behold, the new has come. (2 Cor. 5:17)

And from John's gospel, we hear Jesus say:

> "Truly, truly, I say to you, unless one is born anew, he cannot see the kingdom of God." (John 3:3)

One thing we know from experience is that, at first, new is *new*. It's unfamiliar. Think again about being dropped into a new country or being added to a new family. There is a strangeness to newness. We might want to pretend it's not so. We might want to fake it. But to really flourish in this new reality, we're going to have to learn some things and adapt.

I'm assuming here that we, as settlers, want to receive and take hold of this country – or family – as our new home. Those familiar with the Old Testament might remember that in the wilderness, Israel sometimes provoked Moses, pleading with him to return to Egypt where they had lived as slaves. The discomfort of hunger and thirst aroused thoughts of abandoning God's direction. Instead of turning to God for help, they wanted to turn back. Adapting to the new can be hard and uncomfortable. Sometimes the promise of new and better is so demanding that parts of us become nostalgic for the old and familiar. At different points I have been involved in giving pastoral care to expatriate workers in distant places. For expats working in a new culture, language learning is really demanding. They might be able to shrug off a cultural *faux pas* pretty well, but language is hard. I've listened to the frustrations of strong, bright, capable people who endured being treated like a child just because they had the language skills of one. Thankfully that season passed as their skills improved. Don't let weariness or the residues of your old nature keep you from adapting to the new. Press on into a Holiness that looks like godliness.

NEW IDENTITY

One thing that's new is your identity. Check your passport. You no longer belong in the domain of darkness. You belong in Christ's kingdom. You have a new family. You bear God's name. You have a new pedigree. Your inheritance comes from God and generations of his children who lived before you. It's time to release those old identity markers and to discover the new ones. How do you know what they are? There are dozens of them in Scripture. Look for clues – statements that begin "you are..." or "we are...". Here are a few to start:

- we are loved fully and unconditionally
- we are children of God
- we are the righteousness of God
- we are holy
- we are the bride of Christ
- we are a priesthood
- we are the body of Christ
- we are witnesses of God's work
- we are ambassadors of Christ's kingdom in the world

There are many others. These aren't markers of a *future* identity. They come with resettlement. They describe you right now. This change of identity is by God's decree. Your true identity is *received* from God. It's not defined by friends, employers, teachers, pastors, or family. It's not something you create and shape for yourself. Those identities will be false identities, at least in part. Your new identity might not be something you *feel*. One of the most valuable spiritual disciplines you can practice is to sit quietly before God, Bible open, and ask him to help you discover your true identity. As he does, learn to receive and embrace this true identity. Then live into it. This might seem strange at first. But over time it will grow more familiar.

The Bible shows us many identity markers we all share. The examples above are true for every Christ follower. But that doesn't mean we're all the same. Your true identity and mine are different. There are many things we share but our personalities, our aptitudes, and our interests are personal.

NEW CULTURE

— ❖ —

Another thing that's new is your home culture. In your new life, the patterns of God's kingdom have replaced the world's patterns. You have a new Government, new laws, a new set of manners and cultural norms to learn and adapt to. Again, look in Scripture to find out what these are. Here are just a few examples:

- our every interaction should be an expression of love.
- the least in the world are the greatest in God's kingdom and vice versa.
- power *over* people (control) is replaced by power *under* people (service).
- self-exaltation is replaced by self-denial and self-sacrifice.
- a life driven by the flesh is replaced by a life led by the Spirit.
- expectations of personal comfort are surrendered, and worldly distractions are resisted.

Cultures are layered. People within a particular culture behave in ways that others in that same culture expect and understand. But many times, we don't really know *why* we do what we do. Much of what we do is imitated, not thought out in some logical way. What feels normal to us feels weird to people in other cultures. Likewise, a new kingdom – the Kingdom of God – feels weird to someone born into and raised in the world. It *should* feel weird at first.

Like our new identity, our new culture is received from God. He established his kingdom, and he rules it as a monarch. For comfort's sake, we humans may try to adjust God's ways to fit ours. Sometimes we even add the 'God' label to our distortions. But God's kingdom doesn't bend to suit humans' desires. God's kingdom is as God is. It's an expression of his very essence.

MORE NORMAL, LESS FOREIGN

Becoming a citizen of a new country or being adopted into a new family is a big adjustment. While working with expatriate workers in faraway places, I've seen up close the difficulties of learning a new culture. Smart people [4] have studied migration and have identified four phases:

1. The honeymoon phase. Everything is fresh. The migrant finds every day to be new and exciting. An adventure!

2. The homesick phase. Suddenly nothing works the way it should. The foreign-ness of the new culture is ominous and overwhelming. The migrant's impulse is to return to what was familiar.

3. The learning phase. The migrant begins to see how things work in their new culture. They gain skills, get better at functioning in the newness, and begin to mimic those around them. But there is a lingering sense that the 'old way' is right, better, or more realistic – the way things *should* be.

4. The understanding phase. The migrant is adapting to the new culture at a deeper level than just skills. There is an increasing degree of acceptance of – even appreciation for – the way the new culture

operates. Subliminal imitation becomes more common. Increasingly the new culture is becoming home.

In my work with expats, I have been able to help them anticipate these phases and to endure. You can watch for similar phases in the life of a Jesus follower. A new believer – especially one who was well-aware of their need for rescue – is full of excitement and enthusiasm.

This same believer can become disenchanted with the life of a disciple when they begin to see its demands and hardships. Some of their wrong assumptions about life with God are being exposed. There's still so much to know and they make mistakes.

But those who stick with it – who do the work – begin to see how God's kingdom operates and they begin to adapt with new language and new skills. While they would hesitate to say God's way is wrong, they may still think his way is unrealistic. Their actions say: "We have to use the world's methods to achieve Kingdom results".

Eventually disciples find they have adjusted to the ways of God's kingdom. The Kingdom has become home. The old ways of division, hatred, violence, manipulation, and control have been released in exchange for a deepening trust in God. Christians in this phase are becoming more like their new home, regularly asking God to reveal aspects of themselves that still don't align. It's a life-long pursuit.

Not everyone who enters a new culture chooses to adapt fully. Many find camps of people in their same phase and settle there. Once when working with expats in Asia, I got to know an American physician. In his line of work, he interacted with people who could speak just enough English that he didn't have to learn the local language. He came to regret this because, while he could function at a surface level, he was never able to engage in deeper heart-level conversations. He remained a visitor in that culture. True disciples of Jesus are called to make God's kingdom their home and to flourish there. Their quest is to make Kingdom culture more normal, less foreign – to gradually lose their 'foreign accent'. As with expats, the best way to see this happen is to immerse yourself in the new culture.

The Bible word for *more normal, less foreign* is sanctification. By now you know the Greek word for *holy* means called out or set apart. The word *saint* comes from the same root Greek word and means *called out ones* or *set apart ones*. The word *sanctification* also comes from this same root Greek word. It refers to the process of living into our called-out-ness, our set-apart-ness. Those who have placed faith in Jesus have been made distinct, are a distinct people, and are growing more accustomed to our distinctness.

What steps can you take deeper into Holiness? How can you become more aligned with God's kingdom and release attachments to the world? Can you set yourself in a community that looks more like God's kingdom? Can you surround yourself with people who really live by faith? And can you surrender to God your judgment of – and desire to control – the world's behaviors?

We all need to study Jesus. We need to read and hear God's word (God's message) to know God and align with his ways. We need to listen to God's voice in the quiet and know God's Spirit in stillness. Only then can we have confidence we are imitating the right culture.

During my job as a surveyor, a lot of my work was marking grade stakes for the bulldozers. I didn't mark the finish grade. It was enough that my rough grade gave others a sense of the land's contours. As disciples who are still adapting to our new kingdom, we're not a finished product. But we can display Kingdom culture in ways that others can begin to imitate. What about our discipleship culture helps people understand and envision Holiness? What is neutral? And what might obstruct their view or detract from their formation?

[4] Adapted from M. Winkelman, *Cultural Shock and Adaptation*, Journal of Counseling & Development, 1994

AS EXILES

We have been rescued and resettled. All things have been made new. And gradually newness will become familiarity as we adapt to the way of Jesus. We are a holy, called out, set apart, distinct people. But we're not a removed people. Nor are we superior. We share with *every* person our humanity, God's image, dignity, common grace, and Creation. We remain here in the world. We live here as exiles – beneficial exiles. The apostle Paul calls us ambassadors – ambassadors of another way. We no longer buy into the systems, structures, and patterns of the world. We may have to operate within them (Rom. 13:1-7), but – as a set apart people – we hold to the patterns of God's kingdom.

The world remains – with its systems, structures, and patterns. There are so many who have not placed their trust in God in ways that rearrange their life. Until they do, we can be certain – be unsurprised – that they will place their faith in other things. To say that we are distinct from the world is to also acknowledge that the world is distinctly different from us. We believe that one day Jesus will return, and every knee will bow, every tongue will confess that Jesus is Lord to the glory of the Father (Phil 2:8-9). Until then we should be like Jesus and have compassion on people who wander like sheep without a shepherd (Matt. 9:36, Mark 6:34). I am

sometimes relieved – sometimes challenged – by something
Paul wrote in 1 Cor. 5:12-13a:

> For what have I to do with judging outsiders? Is it
> not those inside the church whom you are to judge? God
> judges those outside.

As a holy people our concern is tending to our own sanctification, personally and collectively, and inviting others
from the world to join us. To carry Jesus' load – his light bur-
den – we have to release illusions of controlling the world.

OUR ANCHOR TREE

Our anchor tree is Holiness. Its canopy safeguards the other trees from intense heat and harsh storms. Its roots stabilize the soil that the other trees share. Holiness isn't a destination; it's a depth. When we give our heart allegiance to Jesus, we become part of a holy, called out, set apart, distinct people. That's how God sees us. But learning to live as holy people is a process. First, we see that we have been rescued from sin and our sins – a governance and an accumulation of behaviors that disregard God's authority. As we take our first steps of faith in God, we are resettled in God's kingdom, and we are made new. We inherit a new identity and a new culture. We acknowledge that, at first, the newness of the Kingdom seems strange. But we make it our goal that this new identity and culture become more normal, less foreign over time. God makes all of this possible by his grace – his gift to us that we don't earn or deserve. Adapting to this new way of life does require effort on our part. Our work is to let go of the old identities and culture (the world) and to work toward flourishing in the new (God's kingdom).

THE FRUIT OF HOLINESS

Trees have a depth, and they also have a fruit. Only God knows fully what the fruit of Holiness is. But we can try to imagine. What if you and I lived consistently as people emancipated from the world's systems, structures, and patterns? Extend that to our families, our local churches, and the whole Church. What if we persistently and thoroughly immersed ourselves in the patterns of God's kingdom? What difference would it make in our own lives if we were convinced that death has been defeated, that we are perfectly known and perfectly loved, that we're forgiven, that we belong, that we no longer need to be concerned about our status in the world's opinion? How would that affect our anxieties? Our sense of self? Our need to win? And our insatiable hunger for more stuff? To me the fruit of Holiness must include Care.

> Cast all your anxieties on him, for he cares about you. (1 Peter 5:7)

The fruit of Holiness isn't just for us. It's for the world too. Like Old Testament Israel we are blessed to be a blessing to all the peoples on the earth (Gen. 12:1-3). How might our depth of Holiness express itself as an offer of Care to those still held by the world; those who haven't yet found the freedom Jesus offers?

Our work, by God's grace, is to cultivate Holiness. We can trust that this work will bear fruit in ourselves and for the sake of others. Just as the depth of a peach tree produces peaches, a depth of Holiness will produce the fruit of Holiness.

The Wholeness Tree

So then you are no longer strangers and sojourners, but
you are fellow citizens with the saints and members of the
household of God, built upon the foundation of the apostles
and prophets, Christ Jesus himself being the cornerstone, in
whom the whole structure is joined together and grows into
a holy temple in the Lord; in whom you also are built into it
for a dwelling place of God in the Spirit.

(Eph. 2:19-22)

A DEPTH OF WHOLENESS

The second tree that defines our farm is Wholeness. This tree sits beside and beneath our anchor tree; its lower, outstretched limbs extending an invitation to climb. Wholeness is about the way each of us relates to all of us. We, a holy people, cannot be whole until we are one – until we experience unity. Like Holiness, Wholeness isn't a destination, it's a depth.

To study the tree of Wholeness let's look at the Greek word *koinonia*. *Koinonia* is most often translated in English to the word *fellowship*. This is a good choice. But the idea of fellowship in our day tends to be a reduced understanding of *koinonia* in the Bible. Other English words that, in combination, help us understand *koinonia* include companionship, partnership, participation, intimate relationship, and life exchange. It's the idea that everyone in a group is fully known, fully accepted, fully loved, and fully involved.

When we looked at becoming a holy people, we were not just thinking about a collection of holy individuals. It's more like we, as a group, have been called out, set apart, made distinct *together*. Here's one of my favorite verses in all the Bible:

> that which we have seen and heard we proclaim also to you, so that you may have fellowship (*koinonia*) with us; and our fellowship (*koinonia*) is with the Father and with

his Son Jesus Christ. (1 John 1:3, words in parentheses added by me)

The apostle John is talking about himself and the other disciples who walked (literally) with Jesus. In verses 1-2, he says they heard Jesus' voice, they saw him, and they touched him with their hands. These disciples came to see that Jesus was Life Made Manifest – Eternal Life Made Manifest. It's this revelation of Jesus that they are proclaiming publicly. Why? So that the hearers might share *koinonia* with Jesus' disciples. And by the way, those disciples share *koinonia* with the Father and the Son. John is saying that proclaiming Jesus as Life Made Manifest will bring more people into fellowship, companionship, partnership, participation, intimate relationship, and life exchange with God's people. And (this is astonishing) we together share this same companionship with the Father and the Son. When I try to picture this in my mind, I see a giant table shared by all the saints (holy people) seated together with God. So it's interesting to me that the word 'companion' comes from the Latin phrase 'with bread'.

In John 17, the same apostle John records for us a prayer that Jesus prayed before he went to the cross. He is praying to the Father for his followers.

"I am praying not only for them, but also for those who believe in me through their message. May they all be one, as you, Father, are in me and I am in you. May they also be one in us, so that the world may believe that you sent me. I have given them the glory you gave me, so that they may be one, as we are one: I in them, and you in me. May they become completely one, so that the world may know that you sent me and loved them even as you loved me." (John 17:20-23)

Jesus prayed that his followers will be one. We are familiar with this concept in marriage: "The two will become one flesh" and "What God has joined together let no one separate". One and never to be separated.

What really stands out to me in this prayer is that Jesus prays we will be one as they (God) are one. One *together* that way. And one *with God* that way. So I ask myself: how is God one? It's a question that leads us to the mystery of the Trinity – one God in three persons. What does that mystery of God look like? And what does it look like for us? There seems to be a with-ness, an around-ness, and an in-ness involved. The word *perichoresis* has been used to describe the Triune God, bringing mental images of the Three Persons in a choreographed dance. I sometimes imagine this kind of oneness in the Church to be like a murmuration of starlings. You've probably seen one. Thousands of birds form what looks like a cloud, moving together, and led by who knows what? Take a minute to look it up. Could this be a metaphor for our oneness together and together with God?

I'm sure every believer struggles with this kind of Wholeness. But as someone who writes from an American context, this feels especially foreign. Not only do we have a self-centered nature – one of the residues from our old identity and culture – but our surrounding culture actively reinforces and rewards individualism.

Oneness – our Wholeness – is not just a nice idea that Jesus had. It really is God's heart for his followers. We must take him seriously. In fact, we see in John 17 that our oneness reveals God to the world. But oneness is an affront to our pride. Those of us who tend to hang back need to show up and contribute. And those of us who like center stage need to make room for others. The biblical metaphor of all of us being members of a body is so helpful here. Every member has its part to play. And members that are typically not seen should receive special honor.

We can make the mistake of thinking that oneness means sameness. Sameness makes oneness easy. Difference makes oneness a miracle. Imagine disciples – with different personalities, joys, traumas, racial histories, areas of brokenness, socioeconomic realities, vocations, hobbies, spiritual gifts, and callings – experiencing oneness in Christ. We actually discover more about ourselves in difference. We are formed even in disagreement.

Oneness is a miracle, but it's also possible. We see instances of this all the time. People who might not like each other very much can find oneness in their shared love for a sports team. While everyone is wearing the same jersey, differences are – at least temporarily – set aside.

We also see this when we are threatened. When people face a common enemy, differences are overlooked until the enemy is defeated and the threat has passed. See, we actually do know how to order our oneness and differences!

If we are truly followers of Christ, all differences must be placed in subjection to his rule over us. The differences still exist. Some of those differences are intended by God. Others may be distortions of God's design. Either way our differences can never be allowed to rise above the Wholeness that comes from our shared devotion to Jesus.

This isn't an argument against denominations, local churches, parachurch organizations, or other groups. Since the time of Moses, God's people have organized in different ways.

But this *is* meant to be an encouragement to commit to a group of believers, listen to one another, learn from one another, and respect one another. In fact, the Bible offers us 59 'one anothers' that we must take seriously. Again, look them up!

As believers we cannot be whole until we are one. Christ's followers are a holy people. We are described by the apostle Paul as a body (let's have no missing parts) and, collectively, as Jesus' bride. We are kin in a reordered family. Peter calls us a priesthood.

Individually we have our uniquenesses: personality, background, experiences, preferences, gifts and talents, etc. These should be seen and honored. But they only find their proper place when submitted to what binds us together – or rather Who binds us together.

We cannot be formed toward Christlikeness alone. We need different ethnicities. We need rich and poor, North and South, East and West, Left and Right, introverted and extroverted, emotional and logical, impulsive and plodding. We need all of these in order to discover ourselves individually and to discover the Church collectively.

What steps can you take towards experiencing Wholeness at a deeper level? We are one family. We are one body. Collectively we are one bride – the bride of Christ. We are one *ethnos* and one priesthood. However we are organized, can the world see God in our Wholeness? What parts of the body are missing? Who is being left out or dishonored? In what ways can you be in *koinonia* fellowship with people who are different, believe differently, or even rub you the wrong way?

THE FRUIT OF WHOLENESS

Again, only God knows fully what the fruit of Wholeness looks like. But we can try to imagine. What would it feel like for you to be yourself, as God has fashioned you, and be fully accepted? What if, even with the distorted parts of ourselves, we were embraced by our Christ-ordered family? As we are learning what it's like to be fully known by God and fully loved by him, what if we could be fully known and fully loved by the Church too? I imagine this would be deeply healing. And I imagine it would be attractive to people outside the Church who feel lonely, isolated, rejected, bullied, dehumanized, objectified, and canceled. I think *Connection* must be an expression of the fruit of Wholeness.

We have already seen that Wholeness is a revelation of God to the world. Oneness is a miracle, unattainable within the world's system in any sustainable way. It's only possible for those who will bow their hearts to Christ. The fruit of Wholeness doesn't look like conformity. It looks like a choreographed dance. It looks like diversity that moves together by the Holy Spirit's direction.

THE PURPOSE TREE

If I speak in the tongues of men and of angels, but have not love, I am a noisy gong or a clanging cymbal. And if I have prophetic powers, and understand all mysteries and all knowledge, and if I have all faith, so as to remove mountains, but have not love, I am nothing. If I give away all I have, and if I deliver my body to be burned, but have not love, I gain nothing.

(1 Cor. 13:1-3)

A DEPTH OF PURPOSE

We are studying each of the three trees companion-planted on our farm: three trees with their roots growing ever-deeper and their limbs laden with fruit. So far, we have looked at our anchor tree – Holiness – and a second tree – Wholeness. Now we turn to our third – the tree called Purpose. This tree is willowy and a fast grower. Some might say it's invasive. Its branches grow vine-like, hard to contain. It escapes every wall. It extends past every fence. There's no keeping its fruit on our farm!

Suppose that we, as Jesus' followers, live ever more successfully as a holy people and as a whole people. Now what? Why are we left here in the world? Is this life just a sentence we have to serve on the way to our ultimate destination? Or might God have something more beautiful and purposeful in mind? I think he does.

For each of our three trees, we have referenced a biblical Greek word. For this tree – that we are calling Purpose – I use the word *agape*, defined as others-oriented, self-sacrificing love. This word has such a sweeping presence in the New Testament. James refers to it as the royal law:

> If you really fulfill the royal law, according to the Scripture, "You shall love your neighbor as yourself," you do well. (James 2:8)

Jesus was tested by Jewish leaders when they asked him what is the greatest commandment. Jesus responds that the greatest commandment is:

> "You shall love the Lord your God with all your heart, and with all your soul, and with all your mind." (Matt. 22:37)

Then he goes on to say:

> "And a second is like it, You shall love your neighbor as yourself." (Matt. 22:39)

Finally, Jesus makes this radical concluding statement:

> "On these two commandments depend all the law and the prophets." (Matt. 22:40)

It turns out that the entirety of God's instruction to Israel was founded on these two commands. Knowing this, a couple of seemingly contradictory statements can both be true:

1. Jesus said: "For truly, I say to you, till heaven and earth pass away, not an iota, not a dot, will pass from the law until all is accomplished." (Matt. 5:18)

2. And the writer of Hebrews said: In speaking of a new covenant he treats the first as obsolete. And what is becoming obsolete and growing old is ready to vanish away. (Heb. 8:13)

To live in this new way of *agape* love is to at the same time fulfill the law and the prophets. Jesus fulfilled the law, and *the way of Jesus* fulfills the law (Matt. 5:17, Gal 5:14). This new commandment to love one another as Jesus has loved us (John 13:34) truly is a noble, royal law! When followed, it supersedes and encompasses the law and the prophets so completely that they become mere shadows in its light.

Our Purpose of love is threaded throughout the Bible. John tells us that God so loved the world that he gave his only Son so that whoever trusts in him will have everlasting life. God's motivation was to save the world; not to condemn it (John 3:16-17).

And there's another familiar passage of Scripture – known to many of us as the 'love chapter' – that's used all the time in wedding ceremonies. In 1 Corinthians 13 Paul describes what love – our Purpose – looks like: patient, kind, not jealous or boastful, not arrogant or rude, not insistent on its own way, not irritable or resentful. It doesn't rejoice in wrong but rejoices in right. It bears all things, believes all things, hopes all things, and endures all things. This kind of love is needed in marriage for sure. It's also needed in the Church – Paul's original audience – and its overflow is needed by the world.

Before Paul describes what love looks like, he strongly makes the point that even when we get everything else right – if love (that looks like this) is missing – we actually get everything all wrong. Can we hear what Paul is saying and receive it as our Purpose?

To be genuine, love must be expressed inside relationship. That means person-to-person and people-to-people. Love only becomes real when it's received and then given. Scripture and experience tell us that it's easy to love people who love us. Even nonbelievers do that. But the uniqueness of Christ-like love is that some death to self, some pain, some suffering, some sacrifice is made to love a person we are not naturally inclined to love. Throughout Church history some teachers have argued that the ultimate test of a Christian's formation is how well we love our enemies. That doesn't mean that we *feel* love for them. The feelings might follow, or they might not. The real test is how we *show* love to others: natural family, Church family, neighbors, strangers, and, yes, even enemies.

ON PURPOSE

Our purpose is to love – love God and love others. To start, what steps can you take to love God more in practical ways? Jesus relates love to obedience (John 14:21). The greatest command is to love God. If we try to love people in ways that disregard God's authority, his word (message), and the patterns of his kingdom, we're off course from the start.

First, we love God. But then our love for God must lead us to loving others. God *is* love. People living in the world's patterns tend to wander – following whatever authority captures their attention. But God designed the universe to operate in a particular way. To ignore God's design is to live against the grain. It brings suffering that afflicts the world and us. In response, our tendency is to control. This impulse to control might possibly be for the world's benefit. People *will* live better lives if they live the way God intends. But we also have to consider that our motives might be more selfish: our *own* comfort. As a holy people who have placed our faith in God, we can be reminded that:

> [Jesus] reflects the glory of God and bears the very stamp of his nature, upholding the universe by his word of power. (Heb. 1:3)

Jesus has everything under control. We trust him. So, can we surrender our impulse to control – and be content modeling an alternative way of living? Can we serve and influence? Can we bend culture toward God's Kingdom in ways Scripture describes as salt, light, yeast, and fragrance? It is more loving to honor people's agency and persuade them than to try to control them.

Every year, around the holidays, it's customary for me to make smoked salmon. A step in that process is brining the fish – packing it in salt. If I were to sit and watch the salted fish for four hours, I would be pretty bored. There's nothing dramatic about brining fish. But when I rinse the salt off, the fish has clearly changed. It has a different texture.

It's the same when my wife bakes bread. She adds yeast and kneads the dough. It would be pretty dull to watch the dough rise. But clearly the yeast has had an effect. The dough has been stretched and expanded. The baked bread will be light and airy.

We are called a fragrance of the knowledge of Christ (2 Cor. 2:14). There's a property of perfume called *sillage*. It's that lingering (hopefully light and pleasant) scent that remains when someone has already passed by.

And if you've ever been in a cave, you know that even the smallest amount of light overcomes darkness.

Each of these metaphors points to a type of influence that sneaks in through the cracks. A kind of bending. It's not at all passive but it is subtle and subversive. When we can't seem to change much on our own, we can trust God and pray. When we encounter greed, we can be generous. When we see people dehumanized, we can honor their God-given dignity. As some ignore the condition of our home, we can be good stewards of Creation. This is what spiritual warfare looks like. It's how hearts are changed rather than hardened further.

THE FRUIT OF PURPOSE

As with our other two trees, we can only try to imagine the fruit of Purpose. What might happen when our roots of *agape* love grow deeper? What might happen in us? And what might become fruit for others? My imagination goes to *Goodness*. Jesus said, "Let your light so shine before men, that they may see your good works and give glory to your Father who is in heaven." (Matt. 5:16) What would it be like for God's people to extend more goodness? Might the Church's goodness attract people to God? Even attracting people to God is an act of love. This is how the Church in past generations got traction – when they cared for sick and dying family members of enemies. And when they built hospitals and schools to serve others. And when they honored the God-given dignity of people at the margins of society.

Is it just me, or has the Church downplayed a posture of extravagant goodness? The Church still does good things, but we seem conflicted – we worry that good works might be perceived as a kind of Social Gospel. Some actually criticize churches that work for good. And at the same time the Church's failures are publicized widely. I think Jesus wants his body's love-as-goodness to be exorbitant, lavish, profligate. Not so that we receive glory but so that he does.

To this point I've imagined the fruit of good *works*. But

there is another kind of Goodness mentioned in Scripture. It's an internal Goodness. Whether you call it good character, moral virtue, integrity, fidelity, or something else, this internal beauty and Goodness must coincide with external beauty and good works. Our deepening Purpose must feed both together. Let the world not just see good people or good works. Let the world see good people doing good works!

COMPANION PLANTED

I have imagined our community as a tree farm. It's a farm defined by its three great trees, companion planted: Holiness, Wholeness, and Purpose. Our successful formation as God's people involves cultivating these three great trees. We want each to grow deeper, stronger, and more fruitful.

These trees might grow independently but they grow best together. Their roots support one another, and their fruits complement each other. Holiness alone can become individualized and removed from the world. Wholeness by itself can become social in worldly ways – us against those who disrupt our comfort. And the Purpose tree, on its own, can lose its connection to God's authority, offering love on the world's terms. These monocultures tend to grow weak, even ugly.

But that's not our farm. Our farm begins with Holiness. That's our anchor tree. We are a called-out people. We live distinctly different from the world. We trust God in such a way that our lives are completely reordered around him and *his* ways. We aren't holy alone. We're holy whole. We are growing deeper in oneness – the same kind of oneness that we see in the Triune God. And we're holy whole with purpose. We exist in the world as beneficial exiles. We're known for our love.

We can't fully know how the fruits of these trees nourish people. We trust that to God. But we can imagine that they might include Care, Connection, and Goodness – within our community and then overflowing to the world.

THE WATCHING WORLD

Those on the other side of the fence are deeply suspicious of our farm. They reject and mock our anchor tree even as they admire its stability and caring posture. They wonder if our Wholeness tree is even real – it won't grow anywhere else. But they seem drawn to its offer of connection and embrace. Our Purpose tree makes them laugh loudest. Its fruit hangs over the fence where they can steal bits of it, with none of their own labor invested. But when they look through the fence, they see multiplied goodness extending as far as the eye can see.

We invite them over and they laugh nervously. But some can't shake the question: what would it be like to live life on that farm? And a few might trust just enough to take a step beyond the fence that holds them in. A few might step outside to freedom.

FLASHES OF YELLOW

At the beginning of this book, I said our farm might be known for many things but its trees steal the show. Our focus has been on the trees. But I can't end without mentioning the butterflies. In my imagination, our tree farm is filled with small yellow butterflies. I live in the southeastern United States. I love the mild winters here, but the summer months get pretty hot and humid. Just when my ability to cope with the heat starts wearing thin, I catch a glimpse of yellow. Did I really see it? Then I see another. Cloudless Sulfur butterflies. When they start to appear, more moderate temperatures are just around the corner. It's still hot but my hope of fall weather is renewed.

Tending our three trees, as beneficial exiles in a hostile land, is hard work. The apostle Paul writes to the Corinthians:

> We are afflicted in every way, but not crushed; perplexed, but not driven to despair; persecuted, but not forsaken; struck down, but not destroyed; (2 Cor. 4:8-9)

Paul and his co-laborers worked hard to see these three trees mature and bear fruit in the early churches. Why were they not crushed, driven to despair, forsaken, and destroyed? I think it's because they were able to maintain their hope: life with Christ forever.

As we do this hard work let's train our eyes to see flashes of yellow. Maybe Cloudless Sulfur butterflies. Maybe sunflowers. Maybe streets of gold. And when some of us are teetering on despair, let the rest of us help them see hope.

We have been rescued and resettled
to share in a companionship of the saints with
    the Father and the Son
where Kingdom life is becoming more normal,
    less foreign
so that the world might know Love.

COMMENCEMENT

If you are a follower of Jesus, you have been rescued and resettled with us. We are a holy people adjusting to our holiness. We are a whole people, learning to move together under the Spirit's direction. And we are a people of purpose, growing in our capacity to love. So now live in holiness, embed yourself in a received community, and be audacious in your love for God and others.

What does this actually look like? Go to the Gospels to see Jesus. Study his life, his teaching, his death. Aspire to imitate him. Then read New Testament accounts of how God's people lived in a First Century context. Move backwards and see God's dream for the people called by his name – starting with Adam and Eve, then Noah, Job, Jonah, Abraham, and the nation of Israel. Read the Creeds. Read early Church writers who were set in contexts very different from – yet strangely similar to – our own. And read modern authors – writers who gather with Jesus and don't scatter (Luke 11:23). Observe the real lives of people immersed in the way of Christ. Read widely from different streams of Christian orthodoxy.

Learn to hear God's message – what God has to say. Prioritize his word above what you have to say and what the world has to say. Then be a doer of God's word, not a hearer only (James 1:22). A Church that faithfully lives out our holiness, wholeness, and purpose will be blessed and will surely be a blessing to all the peoples of the earth (Genesis 12:3). We've been certified by God with the Holy Spirit. So, let's commence.

BIO

Rick Shafer serves as a pastor and faith formation direc-
tor at Port City Community Church in Wilmington, North
Carolina. He and his wife Elizabeth were married in 1983.
Together they are taking in all the joys of grandparenthood,
thanks to two wonderful sons and daughters-in-law.

Rick was trained as a Chemical Engineer and has
worked in the chemical and life science industries. He and
his family also served in missions ministry for a season. His
work experience includes process engineering, marketing,
training, donor development, and member care.

Rick's first exposure to discipleship was with Word of Life
(Schroon Lake, NY) in the 1970s. Since then, this discipleship
interest has been developed and grounded through YWAM's
Discipleship Training School and School of Evangelism,
reading and study, experimentation, and practice.

Rick loves the outdoors – running, hiking, biking, and
swimming. And he enjoys music, reading, writing, and a
good conversation over coffee.

Made in the USA
Las Vegas, NV
22 November 2022

60021253R00044